too fat? too thin?
the healthy eating handbook

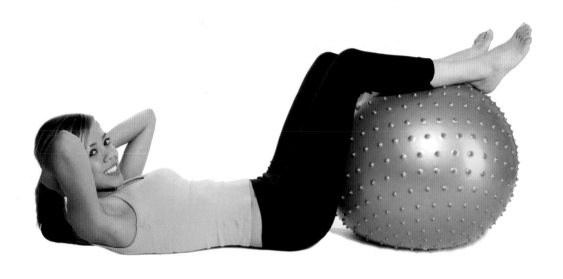

Copyright © ticktock Entertainment Ltd 2009

First published in Great Britain in 2009 by ticktock Media Ltd,
The Old Sawmill, 103 Goods Station Road, Tunbridge Wells, Kent, TN1 2DP

ticktock project editor: Victoria Garrard
ticktock project designer: Sara Greasley
With thanks to Dr Sarah Schenker

ISBN-13: 978 1 84696 957 7 pbk
Printed in China
9 8 7 6 5 4 3 2 1

Picture credits (t=top; b=bottom; c=centre; l=left; r=right):
Getty Images: 25. Sara Greasley and Hayley Terry: OFCb (both), 6, 8, 10t, 13b, 14, 15b,
17, 23b, 26t, 28t, 32t, 38, 41t, 42t, 44t, OBCb (both). iStock: 1, 12, 26b, 28b, 30t, 32b,
34. Reuters/Charles Platiau: 15t. Shutterstock: 2, 4, 5, 7, 9, 10b, 11, 13c, 16, 18, 19, 20,
21, 22 (all), 23t, 23c, 24t, 24b, 27t, 27b, 29, 30b, 31, 33, 37, 39t, 39b, 41b, 42b, 43, 44b,
47. Tetra Images/Getty Images: 35. ticktock Media Archive: OFCt, OBCt, 36.

Every effort has been made to trace copyright holders, and we apologise in advance
for any omissions. We would be pleased to insert the appropriate acknowledgments
in any subsequent edition of this publication.

contents

introduction

Think of a female celebrity. Any one will do. It's guaranteed she will have been in a magazine with 'Too Fat'? or 'Too Thin'? written next to her.

Some celebrities are too thin one week and too fat the next.

Lily Allen has been labelled both in different magazines in the same week. And these are the people we're supposed to look up to! OK, forget the celebrities. Even normal people are on about body size 24/7: headlines, chat shows and even debates in Parliament. Sometimes it feels like we're all going to bust from obesity. Or snap from anorexia. It's a minefield.

Did you know?

Every person is made up of about fifty trillion cells. This book will make you feel better about every single one.

What really matters...

- Wouldn't it be great if it didn't matter about fitting into Topshop jeans? Or having a six pack? If we didn't feel better on 'good food' days?
- Truth is, it matters to all of us.
- So how do we make sense of it without losing the plot?
- How do we sort facts from fiction?
- Work out what matters and stay sorted.

Here's your honest, no-nonsense and air-brush free guide to staying sane in a body conscious world. Find out:

- How to eat right.
- How to look after your body so that it looks and feels great.
- What to do when you're not happy with your shape.
- And best of all, how to accept your body.

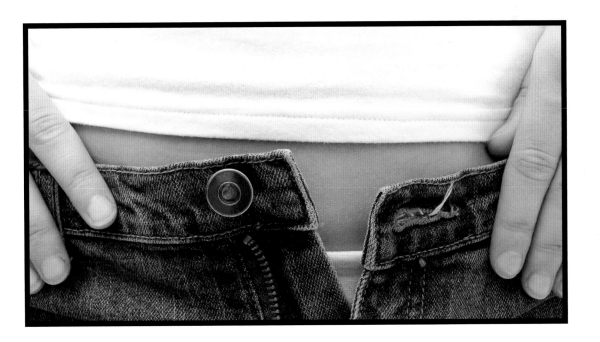

how's your body image?

Body image means how we see ourselves and how we feel about how we look. Take this quiz to discover your body image...

When I look in the mirror I think...

a) Not bad, could look better – but I'm OK.

b) I am totally fabulous!

c) I hate my body and I hate looking in the mirror!

After a day shopping for clothes I am...

a) Happy – I've found some clothes that suit me.

b) Desperate to get back out there – so many clothes, so little time...

c) Miserable, nothing looks good and I wish I were a different size.

You've just finished this week's celebrity magazine. Are you:

a) Irritated. These people are so perfect! You'll cancel your subscription.

b) Laughing hysterically. Celebrities try so hard but look so bad!

c) Upset. You'll never measure up.

You jump on the scales and find you weigh 2lbs more than you expected. Do you think...

a) It's time to try harder. I really should quit the snacks.

b) Chin up. Who cares?

c) My whole day is ruined.

What goes through your mind after a big family dinner?

a) Mum's apple pie is so more-ish, why did I have thirds…?

b) Nothing, except 'Why is it always my turn to wash up…?'

c) I feel guilty and bloated, why can't I stick to salad?

If you could change one physical thing about yourself would it be…

a) Your belly or thighs. Or maybe your height.

b) Not a thing – I am fine the way I am.

c) Everything could be better, especially the wobbly bits.

Answers:

Mostly a's

You feel insecure at times and wish you looked different. But mostly you resist the pressure to measure up to an impossible standard. You just get on with being you.

Mostly b's

Here's looking at you! Wow! Your confidence and security is enviable. How do you do it? Try and be patient with those lesser mortals who fret about their body image.

Mostly c's

It seems your body image is pretty negative. You spend lots of time fixing on an impossible standard and feel bad because you aren't perfect. Go easy on yourself. Try and spend at least a day a week where you forget all about your body and just enjoy it.

I hate my body!

A negative body image is not about being vain or a perfectionist. It's about having a low self esteem and feeling insecure.

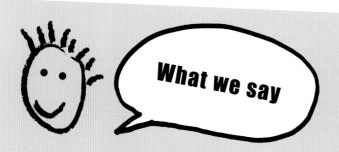

What we say

- "Beauty is only skin deep."
- "It's what's inside that counts."
- "Don't judge a book by its cover."

What we think

How we look seems to be more important than anything else:

- Around 80% of 10 year olds are afraid of being fat.
- The average age that dieting starts is 8.
- Young girls are more afraid of being fat than they are of nuclear war, cancer or losing their parents.
- Women worry about their weight and body shape, on average, every 15 minutes.
- Two out of every five women and one in every five men would trade three to five years of their life to achieve their ideal weight.

So if body image is so important, is it any wonder people try anything to achieve their goals? However daft. Or dangerous…

We risk our health

- A third of British women have taken laxatives or slimming tablets. These cause damage to our bodies which can be fatal.
- A third have tried fasting.
- A third exercise excessively to lose weight.
- All of the above threaten our health in the short and long term.

We splash our cash

- Over £10 billion is spent on dieting and diet related products each year.
- Think about what we could do with the money we save.

Why do we do it?

- Everywhere we turn there are pictures of perfection. Models and celebrities on every billboard, TV station and magazine. Even if we think they are dumb, the message is clear: to be important and successful, it seems you have to be thin. And toned. And beautiful.
- Even if we are happy with our body, studies have shown we become less so after being shown TV ads featuring exceptionally slim and beautiful people.
- Experiments show that seven out of 10 women are more depressed and angry after looking at pictures of fashion models.
- And it's not just the girls. The pressure on boys to be picture perfect is just as bad.

time to get positive

So celebrities are seriously bad for our health. But before you reach for that diet plan or get on the scales, again, hold on...

Here are the official four questions everyone with a negative body image must ask themselves.

1) What does a celebrity have that I don't?

- **Staff.** Including personal trainers, stylists, cooks, make-up artists. They don't do it alone.
- **Cosmetic surgery.** They are cut and sucked and filled into shape.
- **Airbrushing.** No one looks that good. It's impossible. Don't believe your eyes. Just ask any photographer.

2) Who are the important people in my world?

Do you hang out with your best mate because her thighs are toned? Or love your dad because of his six-pack? Or even have a crush on Zac Efron entirely because his butt is perfect? Why do we rate body image in ourselves, when it is not so important in other people?

3) What about poverty?

Is it really OK in the 21st Century to be so hung up on a tiny bit of wobble when half the world (three billion people) live on less than two US dollars per day?

4) What are your best characteristics and what are you good at?

Your sense of humour. Great smile. Ability to complete the latest PlayStation game. These things are much more real. And important.

Time to stop!

Let's all agree it's time to quit:

- Sighing whenever we squeeze our thighs.
- Feeling miserable when we're in the changing room.
- Thinking we're uncool without a six-pack.
- Believing the hype: celebrities aren't all they're cracked up to be.

Instead of beating ourselves up we should take a look in the mirror and be proud. Aren't we looking hot just the way we are?

puberty and body shape

Did you know our whole body shape changes during puberty?

Puberty facts

- We know about the hairs. And the genitals. Half of us get the breasts and the periods, too. But there's a lot more to puberty.

- Puberty starts around age 10 for girls and 11 for boys.

- Starting puberty any time between nine and 14 is normal.

- Puberty lasts about three to five years. In that time we will grow taller by up to 25 cm.

- And we will gain 7–25kg in weight.

Big or small?

The size we end up depends on our:

- **Genes.** Look at your mum and dad. If your parents are tiny it's unlikely you'll be playing basketball for your country. Sorry.
- **Eating habits.** If we eat a healthy, balanced diet (see page 38) we will grow to our full potential.
- **Health.** I'm not talking about the odd cold or tummy bug. Being unwell for a long time can slow our growth, making us end up slighty shorter.

Did you know?

When asked what they would do differently if they had their teenage years over again, many adults said: "Not worry so much about how I looked..."

size zero

Size zero is tiny. I mean really teeny weeny. So small that most clothes shops don't stock it.

What is size zero?

- It's so small that nearly everyone is bigger than size zero when they start buying adult clothes: We go through our natural size zero phase aged eight.
- Size zero is the freakish celebrity who looks like she'll snap if she bends over. Whose head is too big for her shoulders.

The truth about size zero

The US dress size 0 = UK size 4

80 cm (bust)

60 cm (waist)

86 cm (hips)

The waist size is that of the average eight year old.

Size zero and the fashion industry

- The organisers of Madrid Fashion Week banned models with an unhealthy **BMI** (less than 18, see page 24) from their catwalks in 2006.

- In 2007 a model called Luisel Ramos died of a heart attack aged just 22. She had been living on green leaves and diet coke for months.

- So size zero is not just an impossible, unhealthy example for women and girls. It's downright dangerous for the models themselves.

But if I put my mind to it, can't I be a size zero, too?

- Size zero is safe for less than 2% of women, based on their height.

- For everyone else, striving for size zero means, at best, misery, mood swings and endless hunger, and at worst infertility, heart failure and even death.

obesity

Simple to explain, right? We eat more than we need. Do that for long enough and we become obese. No big mystery.

But why do some people become obese when others don't?

- Genes have something to do with it: we are dealt a hand at birth. Some of us can eat more than others and not put on weight.

- Others seem to look at a cream cake and they are piling on the pounds. This is because their bodies are better at storing extra calories.

- Scientists think the obesity gene gave a survival advantage to our early ancestors. Lay down fat in the summer when crops are plentiful and you would survive the bitter winter with little or nothing to eat. Watching your slimmer fellow cave–dwellers drop like flies.

But is this the whole story?

No. Not even close. Even if we are born with the tendency to be fat, we only become so by eating more than we need.

So the real question is: why are we all eating so much?

Over to you:

"We are all large in our family. Helpings were big. We thought we had healthy appetites. Our mum loved to cook and eating was a big deal. It was only when I started having sleepovers with my friends that I realised how much extra we actually ate."

"I started eating more and more when I was bullied at school. The more they teased me for being fat the more I ate. I hid food in my room and comfort ate, trying to cheer myself up, I suppose. It just made me feel worse. The fatter I got the more shy I became and the more I ate. It was a vicious circle."

"I don't think I eat a whole lot, really. No more than my mates. I am sporty and I swim all the time. It's so not fair."

Is obesity a problem?

After all, curves are beautiful. Sexy and gorgeous. And if you are truly happy with yours, maybe it's better to stay that way than beat yourself trying to achieve the impossible. Trouble is, people with obesity have more to deal with than Topshop being a no go area:

- We are more likely to be bullied.
- We might suffer with low self–esteem and depression.
- We get out of breath doing exercise. And our joints hurt when we try.
- We are much more likely to get heart disease, high blood pressure, diabetes and even some cancers. This means we are more likely to die young.

diets: the good, the bad and the ugly

Anyone can lose weight. Stop eating and it comes off. The hard part is doing it right.

Healthy dieting means:

- We don't miss out on all the fun stuff our mates enjoy.

- We don't put the weight back on the moment we're off our diet.

- And above all, we don't get ill trying.

But it's not easy

"I've tried every diet under the Sun. It all goes well for a bit but as soon as I stop the diet, the weight piles back on."

"I eat when I'm stressed and tired. After a difficult day, all my good resolutions go out the window. And if I've done well at something, I treat myself to chocolate on the way home."

"It just seems such a mammoth task. Four stone. That's months and months of saying no to my favourite things."

So why is it so hard to eat right?

Quitting unhealthy eating can seem like one of the hardest habits to break. It can feel like temptation is at every meal time, in every newsagent and at every café. After a rough day, chocolate often seems like the answer. Try and re-train your taste buds: healthy food is delicious. And don't beat yourself up. The odd bag of crisps doesn't make you a failure…

Fad diets

- Fad diets like "The Maple Syrup" or "Cabbage Soup diet" are popular. There is no food to think about. No temptation. And the weight falls off. Big mistake.

- If we try these extreme diets and eat fewer than 1500 kCals per day, our body switches into starvation mode. Our metabolism slows right down. As soon as we start to eat normally our body stores the calories as fat in case the hard times come again. Long term result? Weight gain.

- Fad diets don't teach us to change our eating habits for good. For ever. So we end up resorting to bad habits (missing breakfast, snacking, pigging out at night) all over again.

- We only know we've quit over-eating for good if we can eat normal stuff, same as everyone else. Just go easy on the portion size.

TOO FAT? TOO THIN?

diet dilemmas

When it comes to dieting, it's all about getting the balance right.

"I can't start eating different things to the rest of my family. My mum gets upset if we don't clean our plate and ask for seconds."

It's time to get the family on side. To succeed in anything we need the support of people around us. Explain how you are going to do this right – slowly and healthily. Offer to help with the shopping and cooking. Your mum will come round. She might even join in...

Isn't it harmful to try to lose weight when you're still growing?

Drastic weight loss can be harmful at any age, but especially if we're still developing. Before starting on a diet, ask for advice and support from your family doctor. The doctor may suggest you aim to control, rather than drop your weight. Then as you grow taller, you'll even out. As long as you're eating a healthy balanced diet, there's no age limit to eating right. Set yourself up for life.

Here are your top tips for achieving (and keeping) a healthy weight

1) Exercise burns calories. It also speeds up our metabolism so we continue burning more, even when we've taken our trainers off. We may even get hungry less often and full more easily.

2) Fruit and vegetables are full of goodness and easy to fill up on but low in calories. Make sure you get at least five portions per day.

3) Oats are low calorie and high fibre. This means they fill you up and keep you going for hours without getting hungry again. Pass me the porridge.

4) Snacks. Everyone gets peckish so make sure your fridge is full of stuff like carrot sticks and apples. A handful of peanuts has the same number of calories as five apples!

5) Portion size. There is no reason why you can't have your cake. And eat it. Just be careful not to supersize your meal. (See page 22.)

Did you know?

Most people cheer themselves up with food. It starts when we're little and given sweets 'if we're good'. We all need spoiling, but try and find other ways to treat yourself.

Remember

Anyone considering losing weight should speak to their GP for advice and support first.

portion size

Roughly how much is a portion?

Carbohydrates – eg pasta, rice

- One portion of cooked rice or pasta = size of clenched fist.
- About one third of your diet should be made up from carbohydrates, so have a portion at each main meal.

Protein – eg meat or fish, beans, eggs

- One portion of meat or fish = size of deck of cards.
- Cooked beans = half a cup full.
- Egg = one.
- Have a portion with each main meal.

Dairy – eg cheese, milk, yogurt

- Cheddar (one portion) = size of matchbox.
- Milk = one glass.
- Yogurt = one small pot.
- Choose low fat varieties.

Fruit and vegetables

- One portion = one piece of fruit (eg apple, banana, peach).
- Or a large handful of grapes or berries.
- Or a cup of chopped vegetables.
- Eat at least five portions per day.

Butter

One portion = size of half an index finger.

Shocked? I know I was.

We might think all we've eaten is pasta. But when the bowl is overflowing and the size of a fist wearing a boxing glove, we've actually eaten five portions of pasta!

BMI

Is our weight all that matters?

The right weight for us depends on our height. Our BMI is a measure of our weight, in relation to our height.

Imagine 63.5 kilograms (which is 10 stone). This is a lot for Kylie Minogue who's only 1.53 m. It's about right for Rhianna who is 1.73 m, but much too little for Steve Redgrave who's 1.96 m.

Here's how to work out your BMI

BMI = your weight in kilograms, divided by your height in metres, squared.
For example:
weight = 65kg height = 1.68 m
1.68 × 1.68 = 2.82
65 ÷ 2.82 = BMI 23

What does my BMI mean?

<18.5	Underweight
18.5 – 24.9	Healthy
25 – 29.9	Overweight
30+	Obese

If your BMI is not in the healthy range, your health is at risk. The further outside the range, the more likely your weight is to make you unwell.

The problem with BMI

A word of warning: BMI is not always helpful. Three reasons:

1) BMI figures are for adults aged over 18. Until we've stopped growing it may be OK to have a slightly low BMI.

2) BMI calculations may be misleading in athletes.
   Try this:
   Take Mohammed Ali. Do the maths on his vital stats:
   Height =1.91m
   Fighting weight = 94kg
   BMI = 27 = overweight!
   But he was fit, healthy and it was all muscle.

3) Remember BMI is not the whole story Imagine two friends. Both have BMIs of 22. Perfect, we think. But one is a fitness freak who eats healthily. The other survives on the three c's: crisps chocolate and cigarettes. So there is more to life (and health) than our BMI. It is not the whole story.

how do you feel about food?

Here are three questions to ask ourselves. And some answers that may mean we're messed up about food.

1) Is food on your mind most of the time?

"I plan what I am going to eat every day, before I get up."

"I keep worrying about how much I ate yesterday."

"A good food day is a good day."

2) Does it get in the way of other things?

"If I eat too much I have to exercise to burn it off."

"I'm running out of excuses for not going to my mate's. I can't eat in front of her family."

"Christmas is coming: A big family meal. I am dreading it."

3) Is it affecting your health?

"My period has stopped."

"I feel tired but I can't sleep."

"I am close to tears lots of times."

Sadly, few people (especially women) in the Western World are 100% happy about their weight. Few only eat when they are hungry and never feel bad afterwards. But this doesn't mean we all have eating disorders.

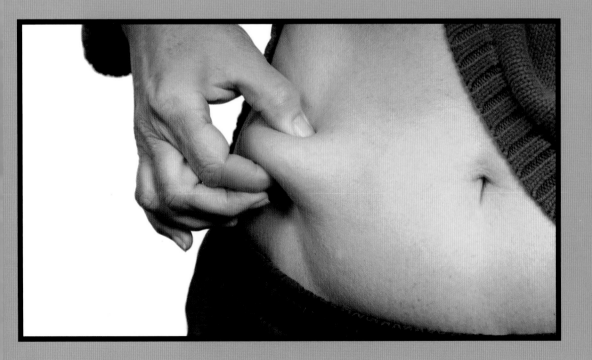

what is an eating disorder?

An eating disorder is when the compulsion to eat or not eat makes us ill. Either physically (body) or emotionally (mind), and usually both. The problem starts when we stop controlling our food, and our food starts controlling us.

There are four main types of eating disorder

Anorexia Nervosa
- An intense fear of being fat or gaining weight.
- An abnormally low Body Mass Index (see page 24).
- Monthly periods stop or fail to start.

Bulimia
- Binge eating (uncontrollable bursts of over-eating).
- Feeling guilty and out of control about food.
- Compensating by vomiting, using laxatives, under-eating or excessive exercise.

Binge eating disorder
- Similar to bulimia, but with no compensating.

Compulsive over-eating
- Eating too much throughout the day.
- Feeling guilty and out of control about food.

Many people do not fit neatly into these categories. We may overlap with more than one type of eating disorder.

could I be at risk of an eating disorder?

Anyone can get an eating disorder, for example a man in his thirties might suffer from anorexia. But there are some factors that might make an eating disorder more likely:

- Being a young woman (aged 15–25).
- Trying to do well at things (a bit of a perfectionist).
- A mum who tries to diet and keep slim.
- Having been chubby in the past.
- Getting stressed about exams and worrying about marks.
- Having a difficult time at home or school.

Scary stats

- At least one and a half million people in the UK have an eating disorder.
- People aged between 15 and 25 are most at risk.
- Girls are 10 times more likely than boys to develop anorexia or bulimia.
- Over 90% of young people with eating disorders feel unable to talk to anyone about it.
- Without treatment as many as 20% of people with serious eating disorders die.
- With treatment the number of people who die falls to 2–3%.

How can I tell if I have one?

Doctors sometimes ask the SCOFF questions:

- Do you make yourself Sick because you feel uncomfortably full?
- Do you worry you have lost Control over how much you eat?
- Have you recently lost more than One stone in a three month period?
- Do you believe yourself to be Fat when others say you are too thin?
- Would you say that Food dominates your life?

One point for every "yes" in the SCOFF questions.
A score of two or more may suggest an eating disorder.

If you have less than two it is very unlikely you have anorexia or bulimia. These questions are only guides. The best way to know for sure is to ask a doctor.

how do eating disorders happen?

For most people, they happen slowly and gradually. They don't wake up one morning with a problem.

- We might start to lose weight and like how that feels so we carry on.
- Over time, controlling our food makes us feel in control of our life.
- The thought of stopping calorie counting becomes terrifying. Even if we know we are damaging our looks, our health and our relationships.

It happened to me

"I started cutting out snacks and unhealthy food. I felt better about myself the more weight I lost. So I started to cut down at meal times, too. I'd find ways of hiding food so that it looked like I'd eaten it. I even tried to make myself sick, but I couldn't. Controlling my food made me feel more sorted in life generally. I would do anything rather than eat 'normally' again. When I look back, I didn't feel good about myself before I started dieting. I was never cool or clever enough. I guess thinking about food and weight all the time meant I didn't have time to stress about other things."

John, 15

I'm worried my friend might have an eating disorder, how can I help?

You may notice they've lost weight. Maybe they're talking about diet and exercise more often. They might pick at their food or even avoid it altogether. You used to stop at the chip shop on the way home. Now they walk the other way.

- Trust your instincts. If you think your friend has a problem, you're probably right.

- It is horrible watching a friend get weird about food. Presumably you've told them you're worried.

- Try encouraging them to ask for help.

- Remember it's not your fault they're not eating properly. And you can't make them stop on your own.

- Be patient. Listen when they needs to talk.

- Speak to a trusted adult about what's going on. It's not blabbing. It's getting both of you some support.

- And most of all, keep your own eating on track. Don't join in...

getting help

I think I've got an eating disorder. What should I do?

You have recognised the problem. That is fantastic. Some of us spend years in denial.

- First, you have to be brave enough to tell someone. Find the right adult and explain what is happening.

- Next, be trusting enough to believe you can sort this. There is lots of help out there: experts who know everything there is to know about eating disorders. People who have helped hundreds of people like you get their eating back on track. They are waiting to help you beat this. The best place to start is with your GP. Ask them for a referral.

Don't be afraid of asking for help.

It may feel awkward or embarrassing at first. You might be worried people won't understand. That they'll laugh at you, or dismiss things as 'faddy diets'. But it is the first step back to being well.

"I was scared to see the doctor. I thought they'd say I was mental and force feed me. But I saw a counsellor and even though it is taking ages, I am getting there."

"I didn't tell anyone because I thought you had to be properly anorexic before anyone paid attention. My weight was normal but I was messed up about food 24/7. I wish I'd done it earlier."

What will happen when I see my GP?

- You can choose which doctor you want to see.
- You can take a friend or relative with you, if you want to.
- The doctor will listen while you explain what is happening and then they will ask you some questions.
- You can ask to see a specialist. Someone who knows everything about eating disorders and how to put them right. The specialist is usually a counsellor. They will help you understand why your eating disorder is happening, help you figure out ways of getting back on track and stick with you while you do.

Most importantly, never forget you are so worth fighting for. You don't have to live this way. You deserve much more and with the right help and support you can get better.

food groups

Unlike car engines that run exclusively on petrol, our bodies are able to run on (practically) any food. We can digest it, process it and use it in some way.

All the millions of different foods that humans eat around the world can be divided into just five groups: fat and sugar, protein, milk and dairy foods, fruit and vegetables and carbohydrates. The trick is to eat the right amount from each group every day. This food chart shows how much you should eat from each group.

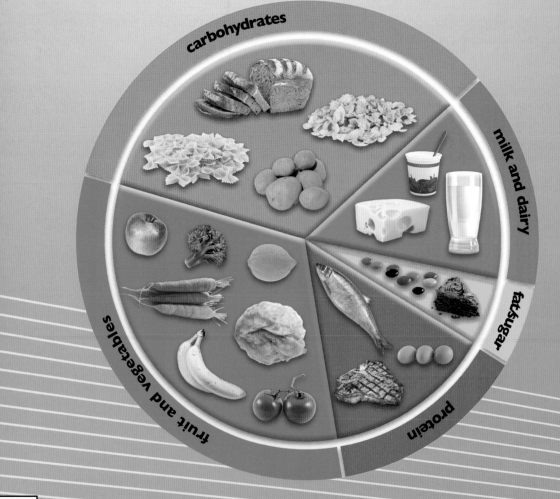

carbohydrates

milk and dairy

fat/sugar

protein

fruit and vegetables

Food group fact file

Fat and sugar   **Eat less**
• All foods high in fat and/or sugar, eg cakes, butter, sweets.
• These foods give us energy.
• Eat only small amounts of this type of food.

Protein
• Fish, meat, eggs, beans and other non-dairy sources of protein.
• For growing and mending the body.
• Try to eat fish twice a week.

Milk and dairy foods
• Cheese, milk, yogurt.
• For strong bones and teeth.
• Two to three servings of milk or yogurt daily.

Fruit and vegetables
• For every single bit of us.
• Provide vitamins, minerals, fibre and energy.
• Eat at least five portions per day.

Carbohydrates   **Eat more**
• Rice, potatoes, pasta, bread and other starchy foods.
• For energy.
• About one third of our total diet should be carbohydrates.

what is a balanced diet?

Our bodies aren't fussy. To look and feel brilliant, all they need is some food from all five groups, every day. A balanced diet means just that. A bit of everything.

It's best to eat mostly carbohydrates and fresh fruit 'n' veg. Make sure there's some protein and dairy but go easy on the food and drinks high in fat and sugar.

I thought calories were all that mattered...

- It's not just how much we eat. It's about quality as well as quantity.
- The recommended daily amount of calories for an average active teenage girl is 2,200 . It's 2,800 for active teenage boys.
- Think of your daily amount as a bank account. You could spend it all on Danish pastries (about 250 kCals each) or use it wisely on a mixture of different foods.
- Invest for the future with a balanced diet.

But my mum does the shopping and she makes egg and chips...

It is tricky if you're eating different food to everyone else. Time to put on that apron and offer to help. Anyone for chicken tortillas? See the British Dietetic Association website for great healthy recipes.
http://www.teenweightwise.com/

Top five tips for healthy eating:

1) **Base your meals on starchy foods** like pasta, rice and potatoes. And go brown. I'm not talking Sun worship.
2) **Eat lots of fruit and vege.** Get AT LEAST five portions of fruit and vegetables a day. There are 7,500 varieties of apple in the world so there is one out there for you.
3) **Eat more fish**, including a portion of oily fish each week. Brain food.
4) **Cut down on saturated fat and sugar.** Grill, don't fry.
5) **Eat less salt** – no more than 6g a day for adults. Stop shaking it on your chips.
6) **Get active** and try to be a healthy weight.
7) **Drink plenty of water.**
8) **Don't skip breakfast.** No excuses. And a packet of crisps doesn't count.

Finally, remember to enjoy your food. A little of what you fancy does you good!

the food lowdown

Ever wondered what they mean by...

...Organic food?

Organic food is made to strict regulations: No artificial pesticides or fertilisers for crops. No growth hormones or antibiotics for animals.

The plus side: Organic food may be better for our health, for that of the people who produce it and for the environment. It may also taste better than non-organic.

The down side: It doesn't last as long (no preservatives) and it costs more.

...GM food?

Genetically Modified food is developed by changing the genes (DNA) of the plant.

The plus side: Crops grow with the ability to withstand the effects of pesticides. They also may be stronger and less likely to rot. So a crop is likely to be more plentiful and easier to grow. This makes food cheaper to produce. This is particularly important in the Developing World where many people are starving.

The down side: Possibility that the genetic changes will pass into other plant species. The health benefits of eating GM food are unclear.

...Fair trade food?

Fair trade food is made with the welfare of the producers (often from the developing world) in mind.

The plus side: It ensures a fair price is paid to the farmers. They can grow crops that will pass from one generation to the next, ensuring their future.

The down side: Can you think of one?!

What is a Superfood?

These are extra healthy foods that may even stop us getting some nasty diseases. There is no ultimate list but most scientists agree on fresh fruit and vegetables, oats, yogurt, nuts and oily fish (like salmon). Go get yours.

Food facts

- The first ever breakfast cereal was Shredded Wheat.
- The average UK citizen eats about 40 tonnes of food in their lifetime.
- There are seven teaspoons of sugar in the average 60g bar of milk chocolate.
- The word cake comes from the Viking word 'kaka'.

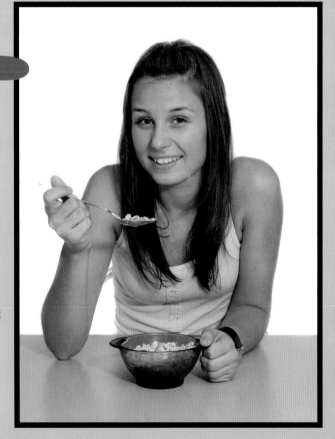

benefits of exercise

Everyone likes curling up with a pizza and a DVD. The couch potato is the best position of the day. But weird things happen to our body when it slobs out too much. Obviously, we fail to look like a Beckham. Or win an Olympic medal. But there's other stuff exercise is good for, too:

Head

Exercise boosts our brain power as well as our muscles'. So we can concentrate. And think quickly. It also makes us happy. Scientists have proven regular exercise is as effective as anti-depressant medication when we're feeling low.

Face

Glowing, healthy skin. What's not to like?

Tummy

Our insides work better if we exercise. Kidneys, guts, womb – the lot. Hands up who gets tummy aches, period cramps or constipation? Here's looking at you.

Muscles

Our muscles get toned and defined.
Name one sportsman who looks rubbish in shorts. Darts doesn't count, by the way.

Bum/hips

One hour jogging = 500 kCals = four chocolate bars. That's the kind of maths we all like!

Bones

Strong bones are a given when we're young. But did you know the health of our bones in our teen years influences how snappable they are when we're old? Avoid a zimmer frame in the future.

Heart

Serious illness. Heart disease. Cancer. Diabetes. Exercise is like taking out an insurance policy. It reduces our risk of getting these nasty illnesses. Bottom line: we live longer if we're fit.

get fit

how much exercise should I do?

- To stay healthy the UK Government recommends under 18s get 60 minutes activity per day.
- That's 10 minutes walking to school, 20 minutes kicking a football at lunchtime, 10 minutes home and 20 minutes perfecting jumping around to your favourite track in your bedroom. Not a problem.

Did you know?

Seven out of ten boys and six out of ten girls aged two to fifteen achieve at least 60 minutes' physical activity each day of the week. But two in ten boys and girls are active for less than 30 minutes per day.

To get fit

Adults need 30 minutes of moderate intensity exercise at least five times every week. Moderate intensity means we get a bit breathless and work up a sweat. Take the armpit challenge: a dry pit means try harder.

Did you know?

Around 30% of young people feel negative or neutral about exercise.

The top five excuses for not exercising. What's yours?

"I hate the gym!"
The gym doesn't suit everyone, but don't worry, there are alternatives. Try the park, local swimming pool or your own bedroom instead.

"I haven't got the time/money."
Exercise for free: ditch the lift and the bus. Take the stairs and walk.
You don't need designer gear.
If Barack Obama, the most powerful man on the planet, can spare an hour to exercise, then so can you.

"It's boring!"
If after the 200th lap of the pool, you're losing the plot, try varying what you do.
Try exercising with a friend or take your MP3 player. That way it's not a jog round the park, it's a gossip session or a chance to listen to music.

"I'm rubbish at it!"
Even Cristiano Ronaldo wasn't built in a day. You are less rubbish than yesterday.
Go slowly, you'll soon get there.

"I'm too embarrassed."
Going public in our gym kit for the first time can be like the first day at school.
It can be tough but be proud. Remember, you're already doing better than 20% of the population who never exercise. Chin up.

glossary

antidepressant medication
Medicine prescribed by doctors to help the symptoms of depression.

balanced diet A healthy diet achieved by eating the right amount from each of the food groups.

blood pressure The force exerted on arteries (blood vessels) by our blood.

BMI Body Mass Index. A number relating our height to our weight.

calorie A unit of food energy.

carbohydrate Chemical compounds providing the most common source of energy in living things.

depression A long term period of serious unhappiness.

developing world Countries with low industrialisation and often poverty and deprivation for the population.

diabetes A medical condition where the body fails to control the level of glucose (sugar) in the blood.

fat Oily chemical compounds that are insoluble in water and high in energy.

fibre The indigestible part of food from plants, which helps defecation (going to the loo).

food groups A classification system for different foods, such as protein.

genes Units of hereditary information made of DNA.

GP General Practitioner, family doctor or primary care physician.

guts The intestines form the alimentary canal, through which food passes.

insecticide A chemical which is poisonous to insects.

kidneys Organs of the body responsible for making urine.

laxatives Medicines which induce defecation.

mineral An inorganic material essential for nutrition.

nutrient A source of nourishment.

pesticide A chemical poisonous to pests.

preservative A chemical used to prolong the life of food.

protein Biological compounds that play an essential part in the working of our body.

vitamin An organic material essential for nutrition.

womb Or uterus. Female internal body organ in which a baby grows during pregnancy.

further information

BMI
www.nhsdirect.nhs.uk/magazin e/interactive/bmi/index.aspx
The easy way to work out your BMI. Please note this is most accurate for over 18s.

Obesity
www.nhsdirect.nhs.uk/articles/ article.aspx?articleId=265& sectionId=1
The NHS Direct website provides information on obesity and how it can damage our health.

Healthy Eating
www.bbc.co.uk/switch/surgery /advice/body_mind/everyone/ eating_right
Visit the switch advice pages. Information and helpful advice on healthy eating.

Diets
www.nhs.uk/LiveWell/ Loseweight/Pages/ Loseweighthome.aspx
Information about healthy ways to lose weight.

Food groups
www.eatwell.gov.uk/ healthydiet
Everything you ever wanted to know about food and eating healthily can be found at the Food Standard's Agency.

Exercise
www.nhsdirect.nhs.uk/articles/ article.aspx?articleId=456
The health benefits of exercise are explained on this NHS website.

Eating Disorders
www.b-eat.co.uk/Home
For information, advice and help on all aspects of eating disorders visit the Eating Disorders Association website.

index